Anonymous

Erection and Dedication of the Soldiers' and Sailors'

Monument in the Army and Navy Lot,

in Mount Hope cemetery, belonging to the city of Boston

Anonymous

Erection and Dedication of the Soldiers' and Sailors' Monument in the Army and Navy Lot,
in Mount Hope cemetery, belonging to the city of Boston

ISBN/EAN: 9783337309060

Printed in Europe, USA, Canada, Australia, Japan

Cover: Foto ©ninafisch / pixelio.de

More available books at **www.hansebooks.com**

ERECTION AND DEDICATION

OF THE

SOLDIERS' AND SAILORS' MONUMENT

IN THE

ARMY AND NAVY LOT,

IN

MOUNT HOPE CEMETERY,

BELONGING TO THE

CITY OF BOSTON.

CITY DOCUMENT No. 80.

BOSTON:
PRINTED BY ORDER OF THE CITY COUNCIL.
1867.

CITY OF BOSTON.

In Board of Aldermen, July 8, 1867.

ORDERED: That the Trustees of Mount Hope Cemetery be, and they hereby are, authorized to present in print a memorial statement of the services attending the dedication of the Soldiers' and Sailors' Monument in Mount Hope Cemetery on the 3d instant, and that the expense of the same be charged to the appropriation for printing.

Read twice and passed.

Sent down for concurrence.

CHAS. W. SLACK,

Chairman.

In Common Council, July 11, 1867.

Concurred.

WESTON LEWIS,

President.

Approved July 12, 1867.

OTIS NORCROSS,

Mayor.

A true copy.

Attest,

S. F. McCLEARY,

City Clerk.

SOLDIERS' AND SAILORS' MONUMENT.

THE INCEPTION OF THE MEMORIAL.

THE sentiments of the citizens of Boston were from the outset warmly enlisted in favor of the most energetic prosecution of the late war for nationality. Her sons were among the very first to proceed to the earliest battle-grounds, and there sanctify with their blood the great cause of freedom and unity. She put forth the greatest and most unceasing effort, during the whole continuance of that mighty struggle, to keep her quotas full; and all classes of the community gladly united in sustaining the common cause to the very last. The families of her soldiers, whose deeds of valor reflected credit upon their parent city in nearly all the great battles that signalized that momentous period of the nation's struggle for existence, as well as of those who laid down their lives for their principles, were ever kindly cared for and generously maintained by the municipal government. Munificent contributions to the resources of the Sanitary and Christian Commissions were never wanting, especially in times of the greatest need; and the hospitality of the city was extended on manifold occasions, with boundless liberality, to those regiments which passed through Boston to their homes after their allotted term of service had expired. In short, it may be confidently asserted that no city in the Union, throughout the war, evinced a more fervent patriotism or a greater spirit of self-sacrifice in bearing uncomplainingly the onerous burdens entailed by a persistent adherence to the cause of loyalty and of right.

In this connection it may not be out of place to mention, in attestation of the above, the number of soldiers and sailors furnished by Boston in support of the national cause.

The whole number of men credited to the quota of Boston amounted to 26,119 ; whilst her expenditures for " war expenses " during the last seven years amount to $2,511,387.50 ; of which large sum $1,947,500.00 still constitutes part of the funded debt.

As Mount Hope Cemetery is the property of the city of Boston, and its affairs are administered by a Board of Trustees, of whom a majority are members of the City Council, it was very natural that they should reflect the feelings of their constituents, as well as carry out their own, in ascribing the greatest meed of honor and of praise to the brave ones who had deserved so well of the republic. It was fitting, indeed, that the living soldier should be greeted with admiring plaudits in Faneuil Hall, and invited to partake lavishly of the city's hospitality, whilst the Mayor and other orators extended to him the most flattering welcome; but those humble men who, mostly " unhonored and unsung," had found their final resting-place in Mount Hope, appeared to the Trustees in office in 1865 to have the strongest claims to recognition at their hands, and they felt their memories should be rescued from undeserved oblivion. A number of these had already been interred in the cemetery; some belonged to other parts of the country, and even to foreign lands, so that no relatives or friends were eager and anxious to cause the record of their faithful life and honorable death to be transmitted to posterity in a permanent form. Their graves, therefore, remained undesignated by any device calculated to remind the passer-by of the fact that the remains of some Union soldier or sailor were there buried, perhaps at his very feet.

Actuated by these views and feelings, the Board of Trustees for the above-mentioned year determined to address themselves to the City Council for appropriations sufficient to enable them to erect a durable memorial which should forever after evince the lasting respect and esteem felt by the city of Boston for those who had died for the Union; feeling certain that the government would not decline to authorize an expenditure of public money in so deserving a cause. It is hardly necessary to mention in this place that these expectations were entirely fulfilled, and that the different requests detailed below were always complied with in the most cordial and unhesitating spirit.

On the 3d of July, 1865, the following order was passed by the Board of Aldermen, and, after having been unanimously concurred in by the Common Council, was approved by His Honor the Mayor, FREDERIC W. LINCOLN, JR., July 8, the same having been presented to the Board by Alderman CHARLES F. DANA, who was at that time the Chairman of the Trustees of Mount Hope Cemetery:

Ordered, That the Trustees of Mount Hope Cemetery be, and they hereby are, instructed to select forthwith a lot in the cemetery in a suitable location, and cause the same to be properly graded and prepared, said lot not to contain less than 2500 square feet, and to be known henceforth as the

"SOLDIERS' LOT."

On the completion of the same, the Trustees will cause the remains of the soldiers deposited at the present time in the lot in the cemetery appropriated for that purpose to be removed to the Soldiers' Lot, and there interred; and a sum not exceeding five thousand dollars is hereby appropriated, to be charged to the appropriation for Military Expenses, for the purpose of suitably enclosing said Soldiers' Lot and erecting a proper memorial-shaft thereon — the same to be prepared under the joint supervision of the Committee on Cemeteries, the Committee on Military Affairs, and the Trustees of Mount Hope Cemetery.

At a meeting of the Board of Trustees on the 11th of July, an offer of a lot of land contiguous to the cemetery, suitable for the erection thereon of a monument, was made by its owner, Gen. HORACE B. SARGENT, himself heroically distinguished during the late war; but at the succeeding meeting, (July 18,) the offer was respectfully declined, the desire being to erect the memorial within the grounds of the cemetery, and any enlargement then not being deemed expedient.

At the same meeting of the Trustees, on the 11th of July, Messrs. SOLOMON B. STEBBINS, HENRY L. DALTON and JOSEPH P. PAINE were appointed a Committee to carry the wishes of the City Council into practical effect; and, on motion of the latter gentleman, twenty-five hundred feet of land next adjoining the lot to be selected for the soldiers and sailors were ordered to be reserved for a period not exceeding ten years for the prospective enlargement of the lot, should the exigencies of the city require it. A lot of land between Greenwood avenue and Heber walk, (as designated on the plan of the cemetery,) was then selected for the memorial lot, and the Superintendent, Mr. CHARLES M. ATKINSON, directed to properly grade and prepare the same forthwith for the contemplated purposes of the city.

At the meeting of the Trustees on the 18th of July, it was voted that the City Council be respectfully requested to change the name of the place selected from the "Soldier's Lot" to the "Army and Navy Lot," and, accordingly, the following order received the approval of the Mayor on the 24th of July, 1865:

Ordered, That the name of the lot recently set apart in Mount Hope Cemetery by order of the City Council as the "Soldiers' Lot," be changed to the

"ARMY AND NAVY LOT."

At the same meeting of the Trustees, it was further voted that the burials in the monumental lot be limited to those soldiers and sailors who die in Boston, and to those comprised in the quota of Boston who may die without the city.

The Committee charged with the execution of the order of the City Council in reference to the monument,

2

at once advertised for suitable designs from architects and others, and subsequently for bids from contractors and builders to do the work required. The Committee and the Board were unanimous in giving the preference for the design to Mr. EDWARD R. BROWN, of the City Engineer's department of the City of Boston, while with like unanimity they selected the GRANITE·RAILWAY COMPANY, operating at Concord, N. H., as the contractors for the erection of the obelisk.

Soon after this decision, the following communication from the Trustees to the City Council was made, under date of Sept. 19th:

GENTLEMEN: The undersigned, in behalf of the Trustees of Mount Hope Cemetery, has the honor to submit the following statement in reference to an order recently passed by your body. The order in question instructed the Trustees to cause a suitable lot in the cemetery to be prepared and graded for the reception of the remains of soldiers and sailors who shall have served in the late war, and appropriated the sum of five thousand dollars for the purpose of erecting thereupon a proper monument. In accordance with the above a space of twenty-five hundred square feet has been laid out in a desirable part of the cemetery, and an appropriate design adopted by a sub-committee of the Board, who also advertised for bids to do the work required. They have decided to accept the lowest of these; but, as it will involve a total expenditure of eleven thousand dollars, they would respectfully submit to the City Council the expediency of appropriating for this purpose the further sum of six thousand dollars.

In behalf of the Trustees,

C. F. DANA, *Chairman.*

Ordered, That in addition to the amount heretofore appropriated for this purpose, there be allowed the further sum of six thousand dollars for the completion of the monument in the Army and Navy Lot, at Mount Hope Cemetery, and that the same be charged to the appropriation for war expenses.

This order was promptly passed by the City Council, and approved by the Mayor, September 25, 1865.

In the year 1866, a new Board of Trustees of Mount Hope Cemetery having been chosen by the City Council, the Committee in charge of the monument was constituted as follows: Messrs. SOLOMON B. STEBBINS, HENRY L. DALTON and CHARLES W. SLACK.

At a meeting of the Trustees, April 26, 1866, it was stated by the Chairman of the Committee on the Monument that, in consequence of the rapidly increasing number of bodies interred in the Army and Navy Lot, it would be necessary to consider the expediency of enlarging the lot, and of applying to the City Council for an additional appropriation to meet the expense of such enlargement. An estimate of the Granite Railway Company of the additional cost for curbing, in view of an enlarged lot, had been obtained, which, with the expense of grading, &c., would make the sum necessary to be procured $2000. It was thereupon voted that the Chairman of the Board be requested to ask the City Council for the additional appropriation named; which was done on the 30th of the same month.

In response to this request of the Trustees, on the 26th of May, 1866, the following order, having been passed by the City Council, received the approbation of the Mayor, increasing the amount appropriated for the monument:

Ordered, That the additional sum of two thousand dollars be placed at the disposal of the Trustees of Mount Hope Cemetery and charged to the appropriation for War Expenses; such sum to be used for the purpose of enlarging the Army and Navy Lot.

In consonance with this order a new lot of land was selected by the Trustees for the Army and Navy lot, and a beautiful and commanding site, fronting to the westward, on the corner of Greenwood and Channing avenues, very near the centre of the grounds, and overlooking Forest Hills Cemetery and the intervening valley, was designated for the purpose. With wise forethought, a space of ground of equal size, in the rear and contiguous to the lot, was reserved for the future needs of the city in this particular should occasion require.

At this time it was confidently hoped that the monument and lot would be in such a state of forwardness as to warrant its dedication on the 3d of July following, — one year from the date of the original proposition for the memorial, and the anniversary of the victory of Gettysburg, a battle most momentous in deciding the nationality of the republic. With this view, the participation of the city government was requested in the services of the dedication, and Messrs. JOHN S. TYLER and DANIEL DAVIES, of the Board of Aldermen, and Messrs. CLEMENT WILLIS, WESTON LEWIS, and CHRISTOPHER A. CONNOR, of the Common Council, were appointed to coöperate with the Trustees in the proposed dedication. It was found, however, soon after, that it would be impossible for the stone-cutters to get their work finished in season for the dedication on the approaching anniversary of Gettysburg; and the services were therefore necessarily deferred till the ensuing season.

On the 3d of July, however, the Mayor, Board of Trustees, the Committee on Cemeteries on the part of the City Council, and a few invited guests, visited the Cemetery and the site for the monument, and were highly gratified at the progress of the work, and the attractive appearance of the cemetery grounds.

It became apparent, as the work progressed, that a still further sum would be required to complete the setting of the monument, grading the grounds, removing the remains already interred from the first-selected lot, and defraying the expenses of the dedication; and accordingly, on the 24th of December, the Chairman of the Trustees was directed to ask for a further appropriation of $2,500 to complete the memorial.

This request, like the preceding one for an increase of means, was favorably received by the city government, the committee to whom the application was referred being pleased, in their favorable report, to speak of "the good taste and economy thus far manifested in the erection of this memorial." Accordingly, on the 4th of January, 1867, the following order, having been passed, received the approval of the Mayor:

Ordered, That the additional sum of two thousand five hundred dollars be placed at the disposal of the Trustees of Mount Hope Cemetery and charged to the appropriation for War

Expenses; such sum to be used for the purposes of finishing the setting of the stone for the Soldiers' and Sailors' Monument, removal of bodies of deceased soldiers and sailors to the new lot, and for grading and sodding the grounds, and dedicating the monument the ensuing season.

Upon the election of a new Board of Trustees in 1867, Mr. JOSEPH P. PAINE was joined with Messrs. STEBBINS and SLACK as the Committee on the Monument, and under their direction the work was rapidly forwarded. The 3d of July, as the Trustees of the previous year arranged, was determined upon for the services of dedication.

At the meeting of the Trustees on the 7th of May, it was voted that the duty of formally yielding the custody of the monument to the Mayor of the City be assigned to Mr. SOLOMON B. STEBBINS, who, for three years had been at the head of the Committee on the Monument, and that its reception from the City in behalf of the Trustees, be intrusted to the Chairman of the Board, Mr. CHARLES W. SLACK. At the same meeting further arrangements were made for the services of dedication by the appointment of the following committees:

On Invitations — Messrs. CHARLES W. SLACK and CHARLES CAVERLY, JR.

On Exercises — Messrs. CHARLES W. SLACK, SOLOMON B STEBBINS and CHARLES CAVERLY, JR.

On Platform and Decorations — Messrs. THOMAS GOGIN and JOSEPH P. PAINE.

On Conveyances — Messrs. SOLOMON B. STEBBINS, THOMAS GOGIN and JOSEPH P. PAINE.

These Committees, with much promptness and success, attended to their respective duties. Special invitations for attendance and conveyance were issued to all the living past Mayors of the City, past Trustees of the Cemetery, the Mayor of Roxbury, the Selectmen of West Roxbury and Dorchester, the officers of the several rural cemeteries in the vicinity of Boston, the officers of the Massachusetts Horticultural Society, the Trustees and Directors of the several Societies and Fraternities having lots within the cemetery, the principal officers of the late volunteer army from Boston and vicinity, and prominent lot-owners; with general invitations to the soldiers and sailors of the city in the late war, and the public generally.

THE DAY OF COMMEMORATION.

The day selected for the services proved one of the loveliest of the season, — in truth, a *perfect* summer's day. The bright sunlight, the warm temperature, the clear atmosphere, — each was complete in itself; while the luxuriant foliage of the cemetery, freshened by recent rains, was one vast tribute, in living green, to the memory of the departed.

At an early hour in the afternoon, the interested participants in the ceremonies began to arrive at the grounds. First came the children from the public schools — sixty-two in number — who were to contribute the vocal music for the occasion, under the

guidance of Mr. JOSEPH B. SHARLAND, Teacher of Music
in the Grammar Schools of the City — in two rustic
wagons furnished by Messrs. POWERS, COOK & COMPANY;
then numerous lot-owners, with their families; large
numbers of relatives and friends of the deceased heroes,
and the residents of the vicinity, generally in private
conveyances. Lastly, by special arrangements of the
Trustees with the BOSTON AND PROVIDENCE RAILROAD
CORPORATION and Messrs. J. H. HATHORNE & COMPANY,
extra cars and coaches conveyed the larger number of
attendants from the city; the former by rail to Forest
Hills Station, and the latter from thence to the cemetery
grounds. It was estimated by careful observers that
fully one thousand persons were in attendance at the
services.

The monument was tastefully adorned with evergreen
and white flowers, the plinth being heavily festooned;
and upon each grave was placed a beautiful bouquet
of fresh flowers from the conservatory of the cemetery.
These last were the grateful tribute of JAMES MORTON,
the florist in charge. All the floral decorations were
under the direction of the Superintendent, Mr. SAMUEL
A. B. BRAGG. At the four corners of the lot, the
national colors were elevated to the proper height upon
staffs provided temporarily for the purpose. The whole
appearance of the enclosure and memorial-stone was
tasteful, appropriate and eminently suggestive.

The services of dedication were conducted upon a
raised platform within a rustic arbor, erected on Greenwood and Channing avenues, to the south and west of
the monument-lot. The green boughs afforded a most

grateful protection from the rays of the afternoon sun, while numerous seats furnished accommodation to a very large proportion of the attendants.

The scene within and around the enclosure was impressive and peculiar. Before the participants was the simple yet elegant monument, hung with laurel and lilies; in its shadow, to the eastward, the eighty-five graves of the martyrs, each strown with flowers; beyond, a background of living green; and the wide borders, on either side of the lot, profuse with floral adornment. On the platform, at the angle formed by the avenues, sat the Mayor and other city officers, with invited guests; to their right, several of. the surviving rank and file of the volunteer army in the late war; in the rear, the children of the public schools, in neat attire, and with happy, interested faces; while to the left were stationed the large concourse of friends, relatives and sympathizers of the departed, with the public generally.

THE SERVICES OF DEDICATION.

Mr. CHARLES CAVERLY, JR., of the Board of Trustees, representing in part the Common Council, announced the order of services in the following words :

REMARKS OF COUNCILMAN CAVERLY.

LADIES AND GENTLEMEN : The duty of presiding over this assembly, on this interesting and patriotic occasion,

3

in the absence of the Chairman of the Board of Trustees, — who participates in the services in a different capacity, — devolves upon me. This duty, though simple, is cheerfully performed. The order of exercises will be found upon the printed programme. Before introducing them, however, you will be favored with music by Gilmore's Band, to which you will please now give attention.

Gilmore's Band of fifteen pieces, who had volunteered their very acceptable aid for the occasion, preluded the services with "Ellsworth's Funeral March," followed by "Roslin Castle," — both of which were played with great feeling, — when the dedicatory exercises were begun by the singing of the following original hymn, by the choir of children, the words being furnished by Mr. SHARLAND, to a *trio* adapted from the opera of "Lurline," by Wallace:

ORIGINAL HYMN.

Peace to the memory of the brave !
Tranquil may their slumbers be !
Peace to the dead, the noble dead, —
Soldier, peace to thee !

Peace to the braves who, resting here,
Gave their lives for rights most dear !
O'er these graves, with falling tear,
We their mem'ry bless !

The Band then played the "Dead March in Saul," after which the Rev. WARREN H. CUDWORTH, Chaplain

of the late First Massachusetts Regiment of Infantry,
(recruited mainly from Boston,) offered the following
address to the Throne of Grace:

PRAYER OF REV. WARREN H. CUDWORTH.

GOD OF OUR FATHERS, AND OUR GOD! We desire to
come into Thy presence, and to call upon Thy name, with
grateful reverence and filial adoration that Thou hast
vouchsafed unto us the privilege of assembling in this
place, to-day, to perpetuate the remembrance of our
noble and heroic dead. We desire to thank Thee that
in the hour of our country's need and peril her sons on
land and sea were not found recreant to the duties connected with her defence and rescue; but that from
every State, city and town, from every village, shore
and hill-side, they started up to maintain, at the
hazard of their lives, her freedom and unity, her rights
and laws.

We would acknowledge, with devout appreciation of
Thy wisdom and goodness, that providential control of
human affairs so signally manifested during our recent
war, which turned the plans of rebellion into fool-
ishness, and brought substantial and enduring good
out of seeming but transitory evil. We rejoice to
believe that when we cried unto Thee during seasons of disaster and defeat, Thou didst incline Thine
ear to hear, and didst finally save our land from
destruction.

Aid us to recognize with profound feeling the obli-
gations we are under to the gallant dead who, beneath

the sod upon so many battle-fields, and under the waters along so many shores, now sleep in honorable graves that we and all future generations may receive the blessings of liberty and union, one and inseparable, now and forever!

Aid us to realize how much of hardship and exposure, of hunger and thirst, of sickness and suffering, of out- . rage and imprisonment, of ignominy and insult, of wounds and death, the privileges by which we are surrounded have cost, that we may appreciate their inestimable value, and see that they are transmitted undiminished to the future.

Accept the act of solemn consecration which has brought us from our homes to this last resting-place of the brave departed slumbering around us; and may the memorial column we have erected on this spot to perpetuate the record of their fidelity, their self-sacrifice and their patriotism, never fail to awaken in all beholders feelings of heartfelt gratitude to them, and to incite others to exhibit the same virtues in their day and generation, to the end of time. .

Crown with speedy and enduring success, we beseech Thee, the efforts now being made throughout the land to heal the wounds caused by the recent sad and sanguinary war. Restore harmony and good feeling to all those who have been discordant and inimical, and hasten the time when the separate States of this great country, united and concordant, shall march on with undivided and unbroken front to the accomplishment of the grand end for which we have been called into being as a nation.

Comfort the families, relatives and friends of those who have found graves in this place, and strengthen them from on high to endure the bereavement which has separated them from husbands, fathers, sons or brothers on earth ; leading all through the influences of Thy grace to prepare themselves for a blissful reünion in the life everlasting !

Speed the Time, O Lord, when the nations of the earth shall learn war no more ; when throughout all lands and across all waters peace shall everywhere prevail, and good-will towards men become the prominent feature of all human dealings and relationships, national and individual.

Command thy blessing upon those in authority over us, whether in the nation, the state, or the city. With especial favor regard the Mayor and other officers connected with the city government of Boston, and endue them with the wisdom requisite to the faithful and fearless discharge of all their duties. May our nation, our state, our city, never lack the men needed to stand by the great principles of freedom, of union, and of universal human equality before the law ; the men needed, perchance, like the honored dead about us, to die for the maintenance and transmission of these principles to posterity.

And unto Thee, O God, will we accord all homage and all praise forever, through Jesus Christ, our Lord. AMEN!

The Band then played the " Daniel Webster Funeral

March," which was succeeded by the singing of the
following hymn, by the choir of children:

A NATIONAL INVOCATION.

God bless our native land;
Firm may she ever stand
　　Through storm and night;
When the wild tempests rave,
Ruler of wind and wave,
Do thou our country save
　　By thy great might!

For her our pray'r shall rise
To God above the skies:
　　On him we wait.
Thou who art ever nigh,
Guarding with watchful eye,
To thee aloud we cry:
　　God save the state!

Mr. SOLOMON B. STEBBINS, Chairman of the Committee of Construction, of the Board of Trustees, was
then introduced, and read the committee's report as
follows:

REPORT OF THE CONSTRUCTION COMMITTEE, BY MR. S. B. STEBBINS.

Mr. MAYOR: The committee to whom was intrusted
the order of the City Council, passed July 3, 1865,
directing the Trustees of the cemetery to lay out and
enclose a suitable lot for the interment of the remains
of the soldiers and sailors of Boston who died in the
war of the rebellion, and to erect thereon a proper
memorial-shaft, having executed the trust committed to
their care, respectfully submit for the approval and
acceptance of the City Council the monument and

enclosure which you, as chief magistrate of the city, have been invited to formally dedicate this day.

From the various designs presented for the monument and other stone-work, the committee unanimously adopted that furnished by Mr. EDWARD R. BROWN, of the City Engineer's department. The lot is situated upon Greenwood avenue, and measures seventy-five feet front by fifty feet in depth, and is enclosed by a massive granite curb, the posts of which at the four corners terminate in a pyramid of cannon-balls. The ascent to the lot is by four steps, with curved buttresses, and posts surmounted by mortars. The path within the enclosure is laid out in the form of a Latin cross, marked by a low granite edge-stone. The monument stands in the centre of the cross, and is thirty-two feet in height. The front and rear die of the pedestal is panelled, the front bearing the inscription:

TO THE MEMORY

OF THE

SOLDIERS AND SAILORS

OF

. BOSTON,

WHO FELL IN DEFENCE OF THEIR COUNTRY
AND LIBERTY IN THE REBELLION WHICH
ENDED IN 1865, THIS MONUMENT
IS GRATEFULLY DEDICATED
BY THE
CITY OF BOSTON.

The rear bears the inscription:

THE COURAGE AND DEVOTION SHOWN BY THE SOLDIERS AND SAILORS
DURING THE WAR FOR AMERICAN NATIONALITY HAVE MADE THEIR NAME
THE GLORY AND PRIDE OF THE NATION. .

ERECTED BY ORDER OF THE CITY COUNCIL:

A. D. 1865.

On the right flank is an emblem, in *bas-relief* of the
army. The left flank bears a *bas-relief* emblematic
of the navy. The city seal is cut on the front face
of the shaft. The monument and curb is of the best
quality of fine-hammered Concord granite, and was
furnished by the GRANITE RAILWAY COMPANY. The
setting of the stone-work was thoroughly done by Mr.
MARTIN L. WHITCHER. The entire cost of the monument and curbing, together with the grading and other
expenses, will not exceed fifteen thousand five hundred
dollars. There have been interred in the lot the
remains of eighty-five soldiers and sailors, whose names,
with their age, and the date of their death and burial,
are as follows:

RANGE ONE.

Name.	Place of Death.	When Died.	Age.	When Buried.
1. JEREMIAH McCANN,	Boston.	Jan. 22, '67.	24	Jan. 23, '67.
2. DAVID SULLIVAN,	"	Feb. 13, '67.	27	Feb. 15, '67.
3. PATRICK DORGAN,	"	Jan. 20, '67.	42	Jan. 23, '67.
4. JOHN KENNEDY,	"	Mar. 17, '67.	41	Mar. 20, '67.
5. THOMAS WELLS,	"	May 24, '67.	23	May 25, '67.
6. CHARLES GILBERT,	"	Jan. 3, '67.	39	Jan. 6, '67.
7. JOHN W. PORTER,	"	Dec. 27, '66.	18	Dec. 28, '66.
8. WILLIAM BARRY,	"	Dec. 3, '66.	40	Dec. 4, '66.
9. FRANCIS L. HARRISON,	"	Jan. 8, '66.	33	Jan. 10, '66.
10. GEORGE F. BOOLE,	"	Nov. 5, '66.	20	Nov. 6, '66.
11. ROBERT WHITSETT,	"	Oct. 19, '66.	21	Oct. 21, '66.
12. HENRY BURNS,	"	Oct. 12, '66.	27	Oct. 13, '66.
13. WILLIAM CARLINE,	"	Oct. 7, '66.	35	Oct. 8, '66.
14. JABEZ J. LEWIS,	"	Sept. 25, '66.	32	Sept. 26, '66.
15. CHAS. E. BATCHELDER,	"	Apr. 25, '66.	21	Apr. 26, '66.
16. JOHN NICHOLSON,	"	Apr. 16, '66.	22	Apr. 17, '66.
17. THOMAS HATHEWAY,	"	Feb. 21, '66.	42	Feb. 22, '66.

Name.	Place of Death.	When Died.	Age.	When Buried.
18. JUSTIN C. DOUTY,	Boston.	Jan. 27, '66.	34	Jan. 29, '66.
19. LEWIS GAUL, JR.	"	Dec. 24, '65.	19	Dec. 27, '65.
20. EDGAR COLBURN,	"	Nov. 9, '66.	31	Nov. 10, '66.
21. FREEMAN FREMUHT,	"	Jan. 15, '66.	22	Jan. 16, '66.
22. DAVID SMITH,	"	Nov. 27, '65.	45	Nov. 28, '65.
23. JOHN Z. LOWELL, Gal'p's Isld.		July 9, '65.	29	July 11, '65.
24. ROBERT LOGAN,	Boston.	Apr. 30, '65.	40	May 1, '65.
25. THOMAS McGUIRE,	"	Dec. 17, '65.	46	Dec. 19, '65.
26. CHARLES HAYDEN,	"	Dec. 18, '65.	26	Dec. 19, '65.
27. THOMAS ALLEN,	"	Dec. 6, '65.	19	Dec. 8, '65.
28. DENNIS DONOVAN,	"	Dec. 2, '65.	30	Dec. 3, '65.
29. JOHN CARR,	"	Nov. 29, '65.	23	Nov. 30, '65.
30. JAMES CHRISTIANSEN,	"	Oct. 28, '65.	32	Oct. 30, '65.
31. G. M. GILLEY,	"	Sept. 30, '65.	21	Oct. 2, '65.
32. RUFUS RAYMOND,	"	July 5, '65.	47	July 6, '65.
33. JOHN HUNT,	"	Aug. 7, '65. .	28	Aug. 9, '65.
34. JOHN McMAHON,	"	June 16, '65.	38	June 18, '65.
35. MARCUS M. SULLIVAN,	"	May 17, '65.	26	June 17, '65.
36. TIMOTHY D. WILLIAMS,	"	Apr. 18, '65.	39	Apr. 19, '65.
37. SAMUEL LIGHTBODY,	"	Mar. 9, '65.	33	Mar. 10, '65.
38. ROBERT LINDSEY,	"	Feb. 26, '65.	26	Feb. 28, '65.
39. JOHN M. RUSSELL,	"	Mar. 29, '65.	37	Apr. 3, '65.
40. FRANCIS RICHARDSON,	"	Jan. 3, '65.	25	Jan. 4, '65.
.41. ORIN C. HUSSEY,	"	Oct. 25, '64.	33	Oct. 26, '65.
42. RICHARD HICKSON,	"	Jan. 16, '65.	24	Jan. 17, '65.

RANGE TWO.

Name.	Place of Death.	When Died.	Age.	When Buried.
1. JOHN C. CARLTON,	Boston.	Dec. 9, '64.	37	Dec. 11, '64.
2. DANIEL R. BRAY,	"	Dec. 2, '64.	24	Dec. 2, '64.
3. CHAS. R. HERVEY,	W. Rox'y.	Dec. 15, '64.	52	Dec. 17, '64.
4. ALBERT GREENWOOD,	Bos'n.	Nov. 12, '64.	29	Nov. 15, '64.
5. OLIVER C. BIXBY,	Out of city.	July 30, '64.	36	Nov. 30, '64.
6. JOHN DURENE,	Boston.	Jan. 28, '65.	21	Jan. 30, '65.
7. JAMES THOMPSON,	"	Sept. 25, '64.	34	Sept. 26, '64.
8. JOHN TURNER,	"	Oct. 25, '64.	45	Oct. 26, '64.
9. WILLIAM McGAWLEY,	"	July 17, '64.	21	July 18, '64.

4

Name.	Place of Death.	When Died.	Age.	When Buried.
10. Patrick Laughlin,	Boston.	Sept. 9, '64.	34	Sept. 11, '64.
11. Morris Carmichael,	"	Aug. 19, '64.	46	Aug. 20, '64.
12. Julius Lorio,	"	May 25, '64.	25	May 25, '64.
13. Michael Finley,	"	July 1, '64.	25	July 2, '64.
14. Edward Brayton,	"	July 9, '64.	44	July 11, '64.
15. Charles Delmont,	"	Apr. 11, '64.	23	Apr. 13, '64.
16. Joseph Patterson,	"	Apr. 5, '64.	36	Apr. 4, '64.
17. James McCormick,	"	May 15, '64.	44	May 17, '64.
18. John Curry,	"	Apr. 16, '64.	40	Apr. 17, '64.
19. Charles A. Dickey,	"	May 21, '64.	28	May 21, '64.
20. Joel Masury,	"	May 18, '64.	43	May 19, '64.
21. James Walsh,	"	Feb. 19, '63.	34	Feb. 19, '63.
22. John Friedrich,	"	Apr. 13, '64.	47	Apr. 15, '64.
23. Daniel McDonald,	"	Mar. 7, '64.	32	Mar. 8, '64.
24. Patrick Gannon,	"	May 6, '67.	50	May 7, '67.
25. William Brown,	"	Feb. 11, '64.	28	Feb. 12, '64.
26. Richard Burns,	"	Jan. 27, '64.	42	Jan. 28, '64.
27. Jeremiah Cooney,	"	Feb. 11, '64.	32	Feb. 12, '64.
28. Robert Saunders,	"	Feb. 2, '63.	36	Feb. 4, '63.
29. Charles J. Doyle,	"	Mar. 20, '63.	24	Mar. 20, '63.
30. Thomas Wilson,	"	Apr. 5, '63.	19	Apr. 6, '63.
31. Edmund Cleary,	"	June 15, '63.	22	June 16, '63.
32. Henry Davis,	"	Feb. 23, '63.	31	Feb. 23, '63.
33. Daniel McFee,	"	Aug. 11, '63.	40	Aug. 12, '63. ·
34. Joseph Higgins,	"	June 24, '63.	22	June 26, '63.
35. Moses Osgood,	"	Nov. 7, '63.	43	Nov. 8, '63.

RANGE THREE.

Name.	Place of Death.	When Died.	Age.	When Buried.
1. John Barry,	Boston.	Dec. 12, '62.	34	Dec. 12, '62.
2. David Richards,	"	June 7, '63.	29	June 9, '63.
3. Charles H. Reynolds,	"	Feb. 4, '64.	38	Feb. 5, '64.
4. James Donovan,	"	Jan. 3, '64.	38	Jan. 4, '64.
5. John Hart,	"	Jan. 15, '64.	23	Jan. 16, '64.
6. Noah E. Barlow,	"	Oct. 31, '63.	26	Nov. 2, '63.
7. James Brain,	"	May 5, '63.	50	May 6, '63.
8. Richard Seymour,	"	Dec. 9, '62.	38	Dec. 9, '62.

Not all of the honored dead who hallow and conse-
crate this ground belonged in Boston, or formed part of
the quota of the city. Many of these men, enlisted in
other States, and returning from service sick or wounded,
found a welcome in our Soldiers' Home on Springfield
street, where grateful hands kindly cared for them
while they lived, and at death brought them to this
beautiful garden of the dead, where they rest by the
side of our own departed heroes. All died for their
country, and are alike deserving of the highest
homage we can pay. We have chosen this anniversary day, so dear to us for the victories achieved
at Gettysburg, as most fitting and proper to enshrine
the memories of our fallen braves. With gratitude
we dedicate this granite shaft to their memory; with
affection we strew their graves with flowers. How
plain our remembrance compared with the lives and
deeds we commemorate! The services and memories
of this hour should inspire us to dedicate ourselves
with renewed fidelity to the cause for which they
died ; and thus shall we most honor and render
undying the name and fame of the American soldier
and sailor.

Mr. Mayor : The monument you dedicate to-day,
beautiful in design and enduring in structure, will ever
express the gratitude of our municipality to the patriotism and heroic deeds of those who fell in defence of
their country and liberty.

His Honor Otis Norcross, Mayor of Boston, accepted the monument in behalf of the city, and trans-

mitted its custody to the Board of Trustees, in the following words :

REMARKS OF MAYOR NORCROSS.

Mr. Chairman and Gentlemen of the Construction Committee: In behalf of the City Council and the citizens of Boston I accept with gratification and pride the monument which you have in so felicitous a manner delivered to me. The work you were commissioned to do was, I know, not an ungrateful task. Your devotion to it, and the success of your labors, are attested by the substantial, beautiful and appropriate structure before us. For the care and attention you have bestowed upon it you have an ample reward in the consciousness of a sacred duty well performed, and in the thanks of your constituents.

Gentlemen of the City Council and Fellow-Citizens : This inclosure has been set apart as a burial-place for our brave men who, either on the land or on the sea, bore the flag of our country in the sanguinary conflicts of the late civil war, and this monument has been erected to mark the place where their mortal remains repose, and to manifest to their friends now living, and to succeeding generations, our appreciation of their valor and patriotism and our gratitude for their heroic achievements. Already nearly one hundred interments have been made in this ground, including twenty removals from the cemetery upon Copp's Hill. Some who sleep here fell on the field of battle; others, after the final triumph of our arms, were returning to their homes in neighboring States, became exhausted from wounds received or disease con-

tracted in the service, and, unable to proceed farther on their homeward journey, lingered and died, after receiving from our people such sympathy and alleviation of their sufferings as their condition permitted; and still others went out from our own city, and, having performed their whole duty in the cause of the country, and witnessed the triumphant vindication of that cause, returned before their spirits departed from earth to meet the welcome of friends and the ovations of their fellow-citizens. The living companions-in-arms of the deceased are entitled, after they shall have finished their mortal course, to the honor of burial in the same consecrated place.

Humbly invoking the blessing of heaven upon our proceedings, we now dedicate this enclosure and this monument to the patriotic and holy purpose for which they have been prepared. The day is eminently appropriate to this duty. It is the anniversary of the battle of Gettysburg; the field where the select of the rebel troops, on a bold and victorious march, were met by our hitherto flying forces, repulsed with great slaughter, and driven to inglorious and disastrous flight. Like the surrender at Saratoga in the war of the Revolution, this was a turning-point in our military fortunes. Soon afterward followed the capitulation at Vicksburg, and then a series of the most remarkable marches and engagements recorded in military history, with victory almost uninterruptedly resting upon our banners, until the final surrender of General Lee closed the eventful struggle.

Four years since a part of the immortal field of

Gettysburg was consecrated as a cemetery for those who had fallen so heroically upon it. In the solemn and impressive ceremonies of that occasion a leading part was taken by one of the most gifted and eloquent sons of Massachusetts, who has himself since gone to "that undiscovered country from whose bourne no traveller returns." His grateful fellow-citizens, whom he has so often entranced by his oratory, instructed by his wisdom, and benefited by his public and private acts, are procuring a statue which shall carry down to posterity the representation of his personal appearance among us. He has himself erected a monument to his memory "more enduring than brass" and more beautiful than chiselled marble.

This hour teaches us important lessons. We stand here over the mouldering bodies of men who laid down their lives that the nation might live, and its free institutions be made perpetual. While we lament the great sacrifice, we rejoice in the advance which has been made in liberty and civilization.

The chief cause of our national discord has been removed, and now let us strive, under the favor of Divine Providence, to make the peace we have attained lasting and unbroken; to allay sectional asperities; to cultivate sentiments of nationality and kindness; to revive our prostrate industry; and to promote by all possible means whatever tends to individual advancement or national prosperity and renown. Let us be as prompt to discharge our duties as to exact our rights, and ever bear in mind that organized bodies, whether political, industrial, religious or social, can insure harmony and a satisfactory measure of success only by charity and mutual forbearance. There must always be differences of opinion as to measures of public policy and questions of constitutional interpretation, but we should never forget that we are one people, whose success, honor and happiness are inseparable.

GENTLEMEN OF THE BOARD OF TRUSTEES OF MOUNT HOPE CEMETERY: With you and your successors in office rests the responsibility of preserving this monument and improving this enclosure, which are now committed to your keeping. The honor of the city is concerned that they shall be protected and cared for, so as to assure the friends and surviving comrades of the deceased who shall in future years visit these grounds that the feeling of gratitude which prompted their dedication remains an abiding sentiment with the people of Boston. It will be your duty to provide not only that the monument shall receive no injury, but that the grounds we have this day consecrated shall be improved and made attractive by such means as good taste shall dictate. The more certainly to insure the constant performance of this duty allow me to suggest the expediency of setting apart from each annual appropriation for the cemetery such an amount as may be necessary for this object. This will constantly remind you of the sacred trust which you have accepted, and be an example which future Boards of Trustees will be likely to follow.

Mr. CHARLES W. SLACK, of the Board of Aldermen, and Chairman of the Board of Trustees of Mount

Hope Cemetery, then made the following response in behalf of the Trustees:

REMARKS OF ALDERMAN SLACK.

MR. MAYOR: The responsibility which you impose on the Board of Trustees of Mount Hope Cemetery in the committal of this monument to their custody is accepted cordially from a sense alike of duty and patriotism. To their eye it is an emblem of the stability and generosity of the city which we love — a token equally of revolutionary renown, present loyalty, and future devotion to liberty and law.

The citizen soldier, leaping to the defence of an imperilled nationality, is the noblest product of republican institutions, for he teaches that all that the wisdom of the statesman and the virtue of the people have devised for the common good is defended with the most precious of offerings, his life. Before us, with the soft sunlight of this summer day alternating with the grateful shadow of the passing clouds, beneath these greenest of swards, flecked with the brilliant hues of garlands, lie eighty-five of these heroes, who took their lives in their hands and went forth to battle for the ideas which our republic represents, and, their duty done, laid them down cheerfully that the nation might endure.

It is no ordinary occasion, therefore, that brings us together to-day to do honor to their memory, while we dedicate the obelisk that shall tell of their patriotism and prowess. Though simple in its details, it yet speaks fully our gratitude. We honor profoundly the men who tendered this great service to their country.

Our eyes moisten as we remember their deeds. Our
hearts beat quicker at the story of their fortitude and
bravery. Behind their self-devotion we discern the
greatness of the hazard involved in the contest. Noth-
ing less than the mastery of a continent, the freedom of
a race, the existence of republican institutions forevermore, were the stakes for which they so valiantly
fought and so nobly fell.

It is not necessary that we should recall the separate
struggles in which these and other sons of Boston
quickened with holy inspiration. Whether those contests were of temporary disaster or full-measured success, we feel that for such a cause as they fought the
humblest effort was an aspiration; every shot fired or
blow struck, an invocation for liberty and right. Alter-
nate success and disaster did, indeed, vary the fortunes
of the great contest upon which they entered ; but we
now gratefully recognize that that good Providence
which guides the destinies of states as of individuals
led us to heights of moral excellence as well as to fields
of martial renown. When we decreed justice to all,
making shackles fall, and enfranchisement the great
sentiment of the war, then was vouchsafed to us — at
Gettysburg and Vicksburg — such momentous victories
that far grander glories than ever before discerned were
added to the natal-day of the Republic.

We stand here to-day on the anniversary of one of
those great successes to our arms when, after three days
of Titanic effort on each side of the contending hosts,
victory, unquestioned, undimmed, and all-reaching in
results, came to our banners. It is now seen by many

5

minds to have been the pivotal struggle of the great contest. With our *success*, the world knew that the nation was to live, and republican institutions not perish from the earth. It guaranteed as long as the nation should endure a home for the oppressed of all lands within the bosom of our continent. It proclaimed louder than the roar of its guns that it is the wisest statesmanship to present in national affairs a great moral issue. It heralded, for the encouragement of the doubter everywhere, that God and Justice on your side are weightier than artillery, and swifter than the advance of brigades. All honor again to the men who fell so heroically with this grand idea within and behind then ! — an incentive than which none could be sublimer ! — contending often better than they knew for the establishment of principles which are now rapidly regenerating this nation, and which, despite old prejudices, are making us a homogeneous, fraternal and all-powerful people. God grant to their perfect enthronement in all hearts a speedy consummation !

But not alone to the fallen are these honors. This monument tells equally eloquently the story of the heroism of those who *live* — scarred, wounded, fatigued — to receive the plaudits of their countrymen. Springing from the quiet vocations of peace to assume the stern duties of war, they have, with like readiness, their task well done, resumed the habiliments of peace. Medals and like insignia may not distinguish them. The uniform of blue in which they proudly marched and fought may be laid aside. Though wanting outward badges of distinction, not less are they cherished in the hearts of the people. They are of that great commonalty of energy, courage, worth, patriotism, and popular power, by which our nation was saved. So gigantic was the rebellion, so vast the theatre of war, so numerous the heroes, that the bravery of even the most eminent almost fails to become individualized in the general review. The traditions of family and the narratives of companions shall do justice to these men. Though occasions and dates may pass from the memory, yet in the breasts of the participants, and in the heart of the nation at large, will it be ever known that it was to the fortitude and devotion of the mass of our people that victory was finally won.

This monument stands, therefore, for the dead and the living in the great contest for nationality! It stands to typify the enduring fidelity of all to a common country. It will receive the earliest glints of the morning sun; the signet of our city's power on its front will hold to the last its parting rays. Beneath the effulgence of noonday, and under the stars of night; in summer's heats and winter's storms; at all times, as seasons come and go,— it will stand, firm, majestic, enduring, to tell of all that was sacrificed, all that was hoped, all that is secured! May it ever inspire the young and strengthen the old to deeds of high patriotism!

Its position, too, is equally suggestive. Of the city, yet without its limits, it tells of twenty-six thousand soldiers sent by the city of Boston to the war, a large portion of whom, not native to its soil, yet sought within its devious thoroughfares the comforts of a home earned as the reward of varying toil. This beautiful valley, with its grateful landscape shut in by these undulating hills, recalls the scenes of their youth to large numbers of our population. Away from the din of the city, the meditative mind finds here that quiet which assimilates so well with noble deeds. These slumberers that surround us, who fell amid the kindly attention of kinship, gladly make room in this rural retreat for those who, from the roar and shock of battle, come hither to share with them the peace of the grave. The numerous company of the charitable and humane who, while living, sought the good of the community, and who, in death, have had pious rites solemnized to their memory, proclaim from tablet and mound that there is no beneficence so blessed as that of a redeemed country. And even the floral· munificence, which now as ever marks these fragrant grounds, by stem and petal, in leaf and flower, speaks from the great heart of Nature to say, Welcome and beauty forevermore to those who die for liberty and right!

The individual history of each of these soldiers for the Union it is impossible here to tell. They represent all conditions of social and army life, — the youthful brave, with the dew of his mother's kiss upon his forehead, early falling in the first assault, and the stalwart veteran, bronzed by four years' exposure, who successfully combated till the final victory was proclaimed. From the first battle at Manassas Plains to the surrender by the banks of the Appomattox, all the principal contests of the war are historied by these sleeping heroes. From the swamps of the Chickahominy and the heights of Lookout Mountain; from the camps of the Potomac, Rappahannock, York and James; from beyond the tortuous Mississippi, along the borders of the Gulf, and all the vast expanse between; from the prison limits of Belle Isle and Andersonville; by the bullet and by the deadly miasma; by accident, starvation and exhaustion; through the portal of battle-field, hospital and private home; from the ships of war that floated proudly at sea or fought gallantly by the shore, — came the shadowy procession of later martyrs that have passed to earthly rest. The solemn roll-call has been heard on every field of renown, and has gathered the host that to-day, in part, we honor. Who, then, shall make up the long list of incidents — filial, paternal, neighborly — that are associated with this glorious company? What tongue narrate the story of each, with pause for the heart-throbs of nearest and dearest that shall beat with the recital? Whose eloquence fittingly voice the great lesson of constancy, suffering and heroic death? The rural town, whose dead of the war are comparatively few, can give these details, so full of sad interest; but the populous city, counting her fallen by hundreds, must be general in its allusions, comprehensive in its description. To the numberless throng, then, whose deeds are unforgotten, though their names are not heard; who abide in fame, though their sepulchre is unrecognized; whose dust far away is mingled with the stranger soil, — pay we now the respect due heroism and merit the most exalted.

The inscriptions which have been placed upon the monument are simple and eloquent; the emblazonry appropriate and suggestive. The art of the architect

and the patriotism of the city have made these silent
stones speak of the past and the future. " The memory of these martyrs ; the noble names which yet have
gathered only their first fame ; whatever good grows out
of the war to the country ; the largest results ; the
future power and genius of the land ; will go on clothing
this shaft with daily beauty and spiritual life." There
are those in this company the mists in whose eyes will
hardly allow the reading of the words or the observance
of the escutcheons borne upon the column. But instinct-
ively they know their full purport! There are those
here, too, who share more than others the inheritance
of fame which the obelisk yields, — the companions-in-
arms of the brave men slumbering beneath! To you
and your associates, my friends, this regenerated nation
owes more than it can ever bestow, can ever even
acknowledge! Great were your sacrifices, but not greater
than the gratitude of those whose hearths, liberties and
nationality you maintained. Your honors are won ; for
" you can hardly be called again to see fields as terrible
as those you have already trampled with your victories."

This monument will have its own history. It will
rank with the inspiration that caused the nation to leap
as one man at the memorable call of the President ;
with that generosity that impelled the tender of means
more profuse than the treasury could accept; with the
patriotism that was vitalized by volunteering beyond the
control of the ministry of war ! It will stand with the
Sanitary Commission and its hundreds of fairs all over
the land ; with the sweet charity of women running
unceasingly from the points of their needles or over-

flowing in stores of comfort and convenience; with the surgings of public assemblies, rallying anew to cheer the army and replete its ranks! It will be associated with the flags of the regiments traced all over with the names of battle-fields; with the returning legions hailed with thundering applause and the welcome of civic magistrates! It becomes a part of the war, — our monumental insignia of universal well-doing, proclaiming a general devotion to the institutions of our fathers! It will mark a new era in the history of the nation, enunciating the theory that only by the entire freedom of every individual is the fullest safety to the State assured; that deprivation of rights to the least of its members is danger to the whole! It will tell of the virtue and constancy of the people, which shall remain so long as the deeds of the past are remembered! Whatever the mutations of time, or the changes of parties; however far we may fall short in securing all to which the great contest entitles us, — we can come up to this edifice from the turmoil of business and political life, and have our gratitude deepened, our loyalty quickened, our patriotism reënkindled! It will thus doubly honor the past and ennoble the present!

Here, then, let it stand! Illustrating a war for union, nationality and the rights of man, it will be honorable to ourselves and grateful to our posterity! Faithfully holding to the principles it represents, we may defy future treason from within or aggression from without; infidel to its inspirations, it will be creditable only as commemorating the virtues of the dead to the shame of the living! With the blood of our brethren cementing its granite, and their bones serving for its foundation-stones, the holiest associations of this hour and presence enjoin upon us loyalty, justice and truth!

The response of Alderman Slack was followed by the Band's playing "Rest, Spirit, Rest!" and the hymn, "Our Native Land," by the choir of children, — the latter as follows:

HYMN.

Brothers, to our native land
Let us vow both heart and hand!
Let it be our keenest pleasure;
Let it be our dearest treasure!
We will ever bravely stand
To protect our native land.

And though many a heart may break,
Struggling for its glory's sake,
Still our pure and holy fire
Never, never can expire!
We will ever bravely stand
To protect our native land.

The Chaplain, Rev. Mr. CUDWORTH, then pronounced the following Benediction:

BENEDICTION OF REV. MR. CUDWORTH.

May God, the Father over all, through all, and in us all, accept the act and utterances of this day and place, and henceforth vouchsafe his blessing unto our country and all her children to the end of time. Amen!

The services of dedication were closed with this benediction.

The large company then sought the various conveyances for their homes, Gilmore's Band generously furnishing appropriate music while the participants were leaving the grounds.

APPENDIX.

The following letters were received from those, specially invited, who were unable to be present on the occasion of the dedication of the monument:

* BOSTON, July 2, 1867.

C. W. SLACK and C. CAVERLY, JR., Esqs.

GENTLEMEN: I regret exceedingly my inability to accept your kind and thoughtful invitation to be present to-morrow afternoon at the consecration of the monument at Mount Hope Cemetery.

As one of the Trustees from its purchase by the city for a period of seven years, I shall ever feel a just degree of pride in all efforts which are made by the city to adorn and beautify the same, and thus render it attractive to our citizens generally.

Yours, respectfully,

BRADLEY N. CUMINGS.

--- -- ------

BOSTON, July 1, 1867.

CHAS. W. SLACK, Esq., Chairman.

MY DEAR SIR: I beg to thank you for an invitation to attend the dedication of the Soldiers' and Sailors' Monument at Mount Hope. Residing out of the city, at present, it will not be con-

6

venient for me to attend, — a matter of little importance to any one but myself.

Having had the honor to serve with you on the Committee charged with the supervision of the erection of the monument, I am happy to congratulate you on the successful completion of this act of municipal duty.

Long after you and I, and our associates in the City Government, shall be forgotten, this granite shaft will receive the homage of millions yet unborn, who will regard it, not merely as marking the resting-place of a few of the brave men who gave their lives to their country, but as an object commemorating the severest struggle for liberty the world has ever known.

Repeating my thanks for your kind attention,

I am yours truly,

JOHN S. TYLER.

COMMONWEALTH OF MASSACHUSETTS,
OFFICE OF SURGEON-GENERAL,
BOSTON, July 1, 1867.

HON. CHARLES W. SLACK, CHARLES CAVERLY, JR., Esq.,
Committee on Invitations, City of Boston.

GENTLEMEN: I have the honor to acknowledge the receipt of your kind invitation to attend and take part in the dedicatory ceremonies of the monument commemorative of the sailors and soldiers who fell in defence of their country during the late war. Having been brought in close contact with the families of those who thus gloriously fell, I have had full opportunity to judge of the cheerfulness of the sacrifices which actuated our soldiers, and the patient resignation of those who have survived them.

My interest and sympathy for those who have suffered is still keen and sincere; and for this reason I regret that circumstances prevent the acceptance of your kind invitation. I am, however, glad of the opportunity through you of bearing my record to the cordial and cheerful coöperation the City of Boston gave me during the war and since, in all measures originated and carried out for the relief of those who suffered in the good cause.

It is also pleasurable to recall the pleasant relations existing between this department and the city government during and since the war, and I thank them for all the kindly courtesies extended to me.

With sentiments of personal regards for the committee,

I am, gentlemen,

Very respectfully,

Your obedient servant,

WM. J. DALE,

Surgeon-General.

CUSTOM HOUSE, SURVEYOR'S OFFICE,

BOSTON, July 1, 1867.

SIRS : I have the pleasure of acknowledging the receipt of your circular of June 28, in behalf of the Board of Trustees of Mount Hope Cemetery, inviting me to attend the ceremonies of dedication of a monument erected by the city, commemorative the soldiers and sailors from Boston who lost their lives in the recent war.

I feel honored by the invitation, and hope it will ever be an honor to the living to honor such noble dead ; and I shall certainly feel it a privilege as well as a solemn duty to be present on the afternoon of the 3d if I possibly can.

I knew the character of the Boston soldiers who fell in this war. As Captain in the 2d Mass. Infantry, I raised a Boston company in an essentially Boston regiment. As Colonel afterwards of the 33d Mass. Infantry, I had four Boston companies under my command. They were like all other Massachusetts men in the army, substantially, and I do not think any greater compliment could be paid them. Massachusetts men were especially relied on everywhere, and I never heard of a case where their commanders were ever disappointed in them; and in all the hard fought battles during the bloody war, where they proved their bravery and their manhood, if one were to be singled out where they especially earned the gratitude of the country I think it was Gettysburg, the anniversary of which you so fittingly select for these dedicatory services. Any one who was in that great battle as I had the fortune to be, could have read in men's faces a stern determination to win a victory there or die. Too many, alas! had to die before the victory of Gettysburg was won. The City of Boston does well to commemorate the loss of such men.

I thank you for remembering me in such connection with my fallen comrades.

Truly your obedient servant,

A. B. UNDERWOOD,

Late Brevt.-Maj.-Gen. U. S. Vols.

Hon. Charles W. Slack,
    Charles Caverly, Jr., Esq.,
        Committee, etc.

Boston, July 2, 1867.

My Dear Sir: I very much regret that a business engagement out of the city to-morrow will prevent me from accepting the invitation with which I have been honored by your committee to attend the inauguration of the Soldiers' Monument, erected by the City of Boston, in Mount Hope Cemetery. No city in the Union responded more promptly and enthusiastically to the call for troops to defend the liberties and to preserve the laws of the country, at the outbreak and during the continuance of the recent war, than did Boston, and the glorious old Commonwealth of which it is the Capital. The Massachusetts men were the first to shed their blood in the maintenance of the laws, and the first organized troops to reach the Capitol of the nation when it was in peril of immediate capture by the rebels. Of the valor, devotion and good discipline of our troops, of their sacrifices, their perils, and the number of slain where the fight was thickest and the danger greatest, impartial history will preserve a record alike honorable to them and to the city and state.

The people without distinction were spontaneous and untiring in furnishing every necessity and comfort for the soldiers and sailors in service and in hospitals during the war; and it is but the common dictate of humanity and gratitude, that every provision which a generous community can make should be employed to take care of the remains, and to perpetuate the memory, of those who perished in the common cause by land and by sea.

No citizen will grudge the pittance of expense which falls to his share of such memorials; and posterity will be gainers by having a spot where their patriotism may be refreshed and their loyalty renewed to the latest generations. It is only necessary, in order that we may have a foretaste of the feelings by which they will be inspired when visiting the resting-places of departed patriots, at Mount Hope and elsewhere, that we now make a brief pilgrimage to Arlington Heights, or the Soldiers' Rest at Washington, or to those now verdant battle-fields, with their cemeteries attached, where repose, in the silence of death, unnumbered thousands of the slain!

By all means, take care of the bodies of the dead soldiers and sailors, and multiply the fitting memorials of their deeds.

I am, dear sir,

Very truly yours,

ALEX'R H. RICE.

Hon. CHARLES W. SLACK,

Chairman.

BOSTON, July 2, 1867.

CHARLES W. SLACK, Esq.

MY DEAR SIR: I trust you will not ascribe my absence to-morrow from the ceremonies at Mount Hope Cemetery to any want of sympathy with the occasion or with the government of the city.

The preservation in perpetual memory of the names and fate of the soldiers and sailors who fell in defence of their country and liberty in the Great Rebellion, — by commemorative monu-ments in our churches and other places sacred to religion or to patriotism, — is most becoming in the survivors, and is a pious service to posterity. *The dead are already immortal.* May the solemn dedication of the monument, reared to the men of Boston who fell for their country, renew the profound impressions of Gratitude and of Duty which belong to the recollection of their career! and may the column which bears their names stand a mute witness, to a thousand generations, of the beauty and triumph of VIRTUE!

The relation I bore to the Commonwealth during the war, and the intimate association I enjoyed with the leading officers of its municipalities, recall to my mind, and prompt an allusion, to the cordial sympathy of effort and feeling, lasting through struggling and weary but hopeful years, between myself and the gentleman who has so recently retired from the mayoralty of Boston, and who must contemplate this monument with peculiar emotion.

I am, with faithful regards, yours,

JOHN A. ANDREW.